LEYLAND SINGLE-DECKER BUSES

HOWARD BERRY

AMBERLEY

First published 2019

Amberley Publishing
The Hill, Stroud
Gloucestershire, GL5 4EP

www.amberley-books.com

Copyright © Howard Berry, 2019

The right of Howard Berry to be identified as
the Author of this work has been asserted in
accordance with the Copyrights, Designs and
Patents Act 1988.

ISBN 978 1 4456 8708 7 (print)
ISBN 978 1 4456 8709 4 (ebook)

British Library Cataloguing in Publication Data.
A catalogue record for this book is available from
the British Library.

Typesetting by Aura Technology and Software
Services, India. Printed in UK.

Introduction

Situated some 6 miles south of Preston, the Lancashire town of Leyland could once claim to be home to one of the largest producers of trucks and buses in the world; a company whose humble beginnings were in building steam lawnmowers in a backyard. James Sumner, the son of a blacksmith, inherited his father's business in 1892. Not having an interest in the smithy, he used the premises to indulge in his interest of building steam-powered engines. Expansion followed when George and Henry Spurrier, two brothers from Manchester, acquired a share in the fledgling company, and in 1895 J. Sumner Ltd was formed when Preston-based Coulthard & Co. purchased a half share. A year later the company changed its name to the Lancashire Steam Motor Company and moved to Herbert Street in Leyland – to premises large enough to accommodate a workforce by now numbering around twenty. By the end of 1896 the first steam vehicle was produced, and by 1899 passenger-carrying vehicles were being produced. In 1902 a further move was made, this time to Hough Lane in Leyland, as a strong order book and a workforce of 150 meant the company had outgrown the Herbert Street premises.

At the 1905 Commercial Motor Show, the company exhibited a double-decker fitted with a Crossley petrol engine. The company still traded as the Lancashire Steam Motor Co. but the chassis bore the name 'Leyland', and by the end of 1905 six vehicles had been put into service. In 1907 the name was changed to Leyland Motors Ltd, and later that year Leyland not only bought out Coulthard's share of the business, but also the company itself. The popularity of petrol-engined vehicles meant that demand for steam vehicles was falling and so steam manufacture was transferred to a smaller factory in nearby Chorley. In 1913 a new site was built at Farington, just north of Leyland, to accommodate the workforce, which now numbered over 1,500.

Leyland were always at the forefront of development and innovation and in 1933 the first Leyland diesel engine for passenger vehicles was exhibited at the Commercial Motor Show, and by the end of the year the diesel engine was available for all models in the Leyland range. Having been interrupted by the war, Leyland's development of an underfloor-engined single-deck bus resumed in 1949. The advantages of putting the engine under the floor were manifold: increased seating capacity, improved supervision of entry and exit, better weight distribution as well as improved access to major components leading to reduced maintenance costs. Joining forces with Metro-Cammell, the Olympic, as it was named, was not a resounding success but paved the way for the models which were to make Leyland the vehicle manufacturing success it was to become. Leyland were also at the forefront of double-deck bus development, and after overcoming initial difficulties caused by noise levels inside the saloon, the first of the extremely successful Leyland Atlantean model was delivered in 1959.

Acquisitions and mergers saw the formation of the British Leyland Motor Company (BLMC), whose market share had increased to a near monopoly within the UK. The bringing together of companies which had previously been in competition, spread over numerous manufacturing sites and with differing working practices, had taken a toll on the groups finances and in 1974 the company needed a government guarantee to keep it afloat. The production of cars was an important part of BLMC's business but the financial returns from car production alone were not enough to support the development of new models without support from the commercial vehicle side of the business, leading to a lack of investment in this sector. In order to protect what was one of the UK's major employers, a team led by Lord Ryder recommended splitting BLMC into separate autonomous divisions, one being Leyland Truck and Bus. While there were no recommendations for closures of any plants, the report recommended a massive capital expenditure from the government, and if this advice was not taken it could be construed that the government had allowed the UK's leading vehicle manufacturing company to collapse, leading to around a million people being put out of work. The result of adopting the report was the effective nationalisation of BLMC. In 1981 the Truck and Bus division was split again, with the passenger division being renamed Leyland Bus, and while being given a greater degree of autonomy, its control was still under the auspices of Leyland Vehicles Ltd. This was to remain until January 1987, when Leyland Bus was sold to a consortium formed of senior management and investment banks. By the end of the same year, doubts were raised over the future of the newly privatised company and in March 1988 the company was sold to Volvo. Initially, Leyland Bus operated as a separate division of Volvo, but in September 1988 it was renamed VL Bus & Coach (UK) Ltd, effectively ending over ninety years of the Leyland name.

This, the second in a series of three books looking at Leyland passenger vehicles, takes a look at the Tiger Cub, Leopard, Panther and Cub, National, Tiger and finally the Lynx. As with my previous publications I have been greatly assisted in my endeavours by a handful of photographers to whom I am indebted, not only for letting me use their work, but also for having the foresight to record these vehicles in their heyday for others to enjoy so many years later. Each photographer has an initialled credit after their work: Alan Snatt (AS), Cliff Essex (CE), Martyn Hearson (MH), Ray Jones (RJ), Richard Simons (RS), Steve Guess (SG) and Terry Walker (TW). Thanks also to Lindsay Jones for supplying the Australian photos, all of which are credited to the original photographer.

Howard Berry
Cheswardine,
Shropshire

The Tiger Cub

First appearing at the 1952 Commercial Motor Show, the Leyland Tiger Cub was introduced into the Leyland range to satisfy a requirement for a lighter weight and more fuel economic alternative to the Leyland Royal Tiger. Initially powered by the Leyland O.350 engine with a four-speed constant mesh gearbox, a choice of single-speed or two-speed rear axle and air braking as standard, it weighed around 2 tons less than the Royal Tiger. Chassis designation was PSUC1/1T for bus use (T indicating the two-speed rear axle) and PSUC1/2T for coaching use, the latter having a dropped rear chassis extension to accommodate a boot. At the same time as the Tiger Cub was launched, Leyland bought a part share in Coventry-based Self Changing Gears Ltd (SCG), and shortly afterwards launched a new type of direct-acting epicyclic gearbox, which was to become the well-known pneumocyclic gearbox as fitted to the majority of Leyland Leopards. The first pneumocyclic box was fitted to a Tiger Cub that was sent on demonstration duties, primarily with London Transport. Over the course of the Tiger Cub's production life the standard engine offered was increased to the 6.15-litre O.375 engine before settling on the 6.75-litre O.400 unit. When Construction and Use regulations were amended in 1961 to permit longer single-deckers, sales of the relatively low-powered Tiger Cub began to dwindle, and in 1969 the last Tiger Cub was bodied by Fowler of Leyland and delivered to Fowler's parent company, John Fishwick & Sons, in January 1970. As the BET group were instrumental in the introduction of the Tiger Cub it was apt that they were the largest customer, with Western Welsh operating a fleet of 271, while north of the border Walter Alexander & Sons took 200 and Edinburgh Corporation received 100. The Tiger Cub was also popular for export markets, particularly Australia, where, as well as vehicles delivered new, second-hand examples were imported from Sweden and the UK.

SARO was formed in 1929 when the founder of aircraft builders Avro took a controlling interest in Beaumaris-based boatbuilders S. E. Saunders. After the end of the Second World War, the factory switched from aircraft refurbishment to building bus bodies. New to Ribble in 1953, SARO-bodied Tiger Cub FCK 844 had almost returned home, now operating with Deiniolen Motors and seen in Bangor in 1972. (AS)

Duple's acquisition of Kegworth-based Nudd Brothers & Lockyer in 1952 and the purchase of premises in Loughborough saw the formation of Duple (Midland) Ltd in 1956. Seen in Bognor Regis depot in 1968 is Southdown's Duple (Midland)-bodied Tiger Cub, 638 (MUF 638). (AS)

South Wales operator Hill's of Tredegar purchased several new Tiger Cubs, including six fitted with Burlingham coach bodies. New in 1955, NAX 537 was the first purchased, but in 1963 it was sent to Willowbrook to be fitted with a new bus body. It is seen parked in Tredegar depot in its new guise. (AS)

Bournemouth Corporation purchased six Tiger Cubs in 1955, including 96 (RRU 901), all fitted with unusual Park Royal bodies featuring a door at the front and an open rear platform. Within two years the bodies had been rebuilt to remove the rear platform. (RS)

Seen at home in 1969 is Leicester 191 (OJF 191), one of four Weymann-bodied Tiger Cubs purchased in 1956. In 1966 they were the first vehicles to operate the original Leicester park and ride service. The large metal plate under the nearside windscreen was used to hold the park and ride destination board. The bus is currently being preserved and is the oldest surviving Leicester single-decker. (AS)

In direct contrast to its brash neighbour Blackpool, Lytham St Annes has long been seen as more genteel and refined. The 1972 Local Government Act saw Lytham become Fylde Borough, and following deregulation Fylde competed directly against Blackpool Transport until 1994, when Blackpool took over the Fylde operation. Seen in Lytham in 1969 is Burlingham-bodied Tiger Cub 54 (367 BTJ), new in 1957. (AS)

The North Western Road Car Company operated across Cheshire, Lancashire, Yorkshire, Derbyshire and Staffordshire. In 1969, control of NWRCC passed to the National Bus Company, and in 1972 the company was split, with part of the Cheshire operations passing to Crosville. Seen in Altrincham shortly after the split and already painted in full Crosville livery is Willowbrook-bodied Tiger Cub STL915 (LDB 774). (AS)

Tudor Williams, trading as Pioneer of Laugharne, operated several second-hand Tiger Cubs, including long withdrawn Harrington-bodied PMW 386. New in 1958, the distinctive peaked dome indicates that it was new to Silver Star of Porton Down, passing from them to Wilts & Dorset, whose name can be seen through the flaking paint on the destination display. (RS)

George Summerson commenced bus operations in 1927 with a fourteen-seat Chevrolet. He was later joined by his brother William, and the new business started using the fleetname 'The Eden'. In 1995 The Eden was acquired by United Automobile Services Ltd and became a part of the Arriva Group plc. Leyland vehicles featured strongly in the fleet, including Plaxton-bodied Tiger Cub YPT 341, which was new in 1958. (AS)

Looking extremely tidy for its fourteen years is Metro-Cammell-bodied YAL 374, one of nearly ninety Tiger Cubs bought by East Midland Motor Service between 1954 and 1961. By 1972 it had received NBC livery and is seen outside Chesterfield depot alongside the company's AEC Matador recovery vehicle. (TW)

Formed in 1920, Cardiff-based Western Welsh's operating territory spread across not only most of South Wales, but also into the western parts of England. They were one of the first operators to order the Tiger Cub and went on to become the UK's biggest purchaser. With Western Welsh's headquarters forming an impressive backdrop, MUH 154 waits in Cardiff bus station. (RS)

In 1958, West Bromwich Corporation took delivery of three Tiger Cubs with unusual rear entrance bodywork by Birmingham-based Mulliner. They were also the only examples of the rare 7-foot 6-inch-wide PSUC1/4 version delivered to a municipal fleet. In 1969, West Brom's buses, along with those of Birmingham, Walsall and Wolverhampton, became part of West Midlands PTE. 213 (UEA 213) is seen inside Oak Lane depot just prior to the transfer. (AS)

Davies Bros of Pencader were another independent operator to purchase new Tiger Cubs, including the last coach-bodied example delivered to a UK operator. An earlier delivery was 51 (NBX 581), which was fitted with a rather elegant Willowbrook body and served the company for over twenty years. (RS)

Neighbours Mexborough & Swinton Traction Company and Yorkshire Traction were both controlled by the BET (British Electric Traction Co.), and when the NBC was formed, Mexborough & Swinton was absorbed into Yorkshire Traction. Mexborough & Swinton's 55 (YWT 55), a 1959 Weymann-bodied Tiger Cub, is seen carrying a healthy load at Sheffield Pond Street bus station on a dismal January day in 1969. (AS)

For over fifty years, Robert Chisnell's King Alfred Motor Services provided a network of stage carriage services from their base in Winchester. A combination of rising costs and reducing passenger numbers saw the company sold to NBC subsidiary Hants & Dorset in 1973. Seen in the Broadway, Winchester, a year before closure is Weymann-bodied Tiger Cub WCG 105, one of nine purchased new by the company. (AS)

Ringway Airport, the original name of what is now Manchester International Airport, would have been a fair trip to make onboard Potteries' Willowbrook-bodied Tiger Cub 402 (2742 AC), it being a good 40 miles from Stoke-on-Trent. New to Stratford Blue in 1960, the bus is seen at Clough Street depot, Hanley, in 1971. (AS)

With over 200 buses, Rhondda Transport was once Wales' largest bus operator. In 1971, Rhondda was taken over by Western Welsh, who subsequently merged with Red & White to form NBC subsidiary National Welsh. Rhondda's Weymann-bodied Tiger Cub XTG 367 became U4859 in the Western Welsh fleet and is seen in Bridgend bus station in 1974. (AS)

One of the Forest of Dean's most interesting bus operators was Soudley Valley of Cinderford, formed in 1928 by brothers Fred and Roy Bevan. In 1979, Soudley Valley transported my school class from Bristol to the Forest and a word with the driver resulted in a visit to the depot. Parked in a shed was Willowbrook-bodied Tiger Cub WDF 569, seen here when new twenty years earlier. Thankfully it survived and is now superbly restored. (AS)

While the Tiger Cub was popular in England and Wales, it didn't sell as well north of the border, with only Walter Alexander and Edinburgh Corporation taking any real numbers. Edinburgh's 100 all had semi-automatic pneumocyclic gearboxes, making them the biggest fleet to be so fitted. New in 1960, Weymann-bodied 95 (VSC 95) is seen in Princes Street, Edinburgh, in 1971. (AS)

One of Lancashire's dark 'satanic' mills towers over Rossendale Corporation's East Lancs-bodied Tiger Cub, 59 (738 NTD). The bus was new to Rawtenstall Corporation, as was the East Lancs-bodied Leyland PD3 behind. Rawtenstall's general manager had responsibility for the operations of neighbouring Haslingden Corporation and Ramsbottom UDC. All remained separate organisations until 1968, when Rawtenstsall and Haslingden formed the Rossendale Joint Transport Committee, Ramsbottom becoming part of SELNEC PTE. (RS)

The smart green and white buses of Dan Jones of Carmarthen were a familiar sight in west Wales until the fleet was taken over by Davies of Pencader. Many of Jones' buses were bought brand new, with Bristols and Bedfords being favoured. A second-hand purchase was ex-Stratford Blue Park Royal-bodied Tiger Cub 3945 UE, seen picking up in Carmarthen bus station. (RS)

Rugged and economical, second-hand Tiger Cubs were useful for non-PSV use. Building contractor George Wimpey had a sizeable fleet of buses to transport workers between sites. Seen on Wandsworth High Street in 1972 when just eleven years old is ex-Southdown Marshall-bodied 7657 CD. (AS)

A stylish change from the Weymann-bodied Tiger Cubs is Alexander dual-purpose-bodied YRC 181. Owned by Trent, it was on hire to North Western when photographed in Stockport's Mersey Square in 1970. When North Western was split four ways in 1972, its depots in Matlock and Leek passed to Trent. (AS)

Originally fitted with an Alexander body similar to that in the previous picture, Yorkshire Traction's WHE 212 was rebodied in 1963 with another Alexander body, this time a Y type. Seen outside Shafton depot in Barnsley, it was the only Y-type-bodied Tiger Cub in the Yorkshire Traction fleet. (RS)

For many years Doncaster Corporation Transport maintained and operated two buses on behalf of the Education Department. These buses, lettered A and B, were used to carry children with special needs to and from school, as well as provided transport to and from swimming baths. When this photograph was taken, the two vehicles were 434/435 MDT, Roe-bodied Tiger Cubs formerly numbered 34 and 35 in the Doncaster fleet. (RS)

Rhondda's fleet was red, or at least it was until 1967. After Rhondda and Western Welsh came under common ownership in 1966, Rhondda followed Western Welsh in having a different livery for their coach fleet. In 1967, the first vehicle to appear in the new green and cream livery was Willowbrook dual-purpose-bodied Tiger Cub 393 WTG. (CE)

A wonderful nostalgic shot of the days when televisions were rented rather than bought and bus drivers wore caps. The driver on Western Welsh's Willowbrook-bodied Tiger Cub ABO 327B gives the photographer a big smile as he departs Newport bus station in 1969. Having departed this bus station on many occasions myself, I can't say I blame him. (AS)

The standard BET-style body was built by a number of bodybuilders but to basically the same design, incorporating the BET-style curved windscreen. Crosville's STL935 (DBO 351C) is a 1965 Marshall-bodied Tiger Cub seen outside Aberystwyth depot in 1972 (note the Crosville name written across the roof of the depot). And if you were wondering about the window rubbers, yes they are red, as the bus was new to Western Welsh. (AS)

The initial formation of SELNEC (South East Lancashire, North East Cheshire) PTE brought together eleven of North West England's municipal or corporation bus fleets, split into three divisions based on geographical area. Oldham Corporation became part of SELNEC (Southern), and 15 (115 JBU) with bodywork by Seddon Motors subsidiary Pennine Coachcraft is seen inside Oldham depot. (RS)

JFK.727 was one of two dual-door Comeng Vehicle Industries (CVI)-bodied Tiger Cubs delivered new to Eastern Suburbs Bus Services of Caulfield, but when this photograph was taken had passed to Sinclair's Bus Service of Melbourne. It is seen at the wonderfully named Batman Avenue tram terminus in Melbourne, with one of the city's trams just visible in the background. (LJ)

As mentioned earlier, the Tiger Cub had relatively few customers north of the border. Despite the Albion Aberdonian (a lightweight alternative to the Tiger Cub) being named after the good people of the Granite City, Aberdeen Corporation purchased none, instead taking twelve Tiger Cubs split between two batches. All were fitted with dual-door Alexander Y-type bodies, as seen on ERG 5D parked in King Street garage in 1971. (AS)

Leyland-based John Fishwick & Sons was formed in 1907 with a steam waggon bought from the Leyland factory. The first passenger vehicle arrived in 1910 and until 1963 only Leyland chassis entered the fleet, most fitted with Leyland-built bodies. YTE 951D was a Massey-bodied Tiger Cub, seen at the old Fox Street bus station in Preston in 1969. (AS)

Blackburn Corporation's first motor buses appeared in 1929, previous vehicles being trams powered by steam or electric. Under the 1972 Local Government Act, neighbouring Darwen Corporation's buses were merged into the Blackburn fleet, which remained under local control until sold to Transdev Blazefield in 2006. The twenty East Lancs-bodied Tiger Cubs delivered in 1967/8, including 64 (LCB 64G), were among the last Tiger Cubs delivered to a UK operator and the first single-deckers to enter the fleet since 1947. (RS)

On hire to Stonier's of Goldenhill is Lancashire United's Marshall-bodied ETJ 127F. Its leisurely progress and manual gearbox did nothing to enhance its popularity with Stonier's drivers, but travelling downhill allegedly improved the top speed. So it was that one unfortunate morning ETJ came racing over the top of Limekiln Bank in Bucknall, straight into the back of a lorry waiting at the traffic lights. Its 'professional' destination board was one of many created by photographer MH during his time at Stonier's. (MH)

While the NBC consisted predominantly of former BET and THC fleets, a small number of independents were brought into the fold. In April 1969, the family controlled Welsh independent Jones of Aberbeeg was sold to the NBC, together with over forty vehicles. Jones's vehicles were among the small number of NBC vehicles painted blue and remained so until 1979, a year after Jones, Red & White and Western Welsh became National Welsh. Willowbrook-bodied Tiger Cub OWO 756F, still retaining its original Jones destination glass, is seen parked at Aberbeeg. (RS)

For many years A. E. & F. R. Brewer of Caerau was predominantly AEC; indeed, when this photograph was taken there were only two Leylands in the fleet. It seems surprising that in view of the terrain of their operating areas, South Welsh operators favoured the low-powered Tiger Cub, taking most of the final build between them. The driver of Willowbrook-bodied WTX 334H pulls hard on the steering wheel as he prepares for departure from Maesteg. (MH)

There seems nothing unusual about YAX 474J leaving the Coal Board offices at Ystrad Mynach until you realise that Tiger Cub production ended in 1968 and 'J' was a 1971 year suffix. YAX 474J was rebuilt from former Grey Green Harrington-bodied Leyland Tiger Cub SJJ 304 and rebodied by Willowbrook for R. I. Davies of Tredegar. The rebuild used parts from Jones of Aberbeeg Willowbrook-bodied Leyland Leopard LWO 319E, which was written off after a serious accident. Let's hope that the advertised express service to the Belgian coast wasn't undertaken on the Tiger Cub! (TW)

South Western Coach Lines had depots in Revesby and Jannali in Sydney. They purchased a batch of ex-Metropolitan Transport Trust Tiger Cubs in the mid-1980s. One was MO 707, fitted with a Howard Porter body. It is seen in South Terrace, Bankstown station, having just completed route 38 from Revesby Heights via Bankstown Hospital. (Norman Chambers)

The Leopard

At the Scottish Motor Show in 1959, Leyland unveiled its new medium-weight chassis: the Leopard. Two versions were shown: the L1, with a straight chassis frame and intended primarily for bus work, and the L2, with a stepped rear frame and two-speed axle, and which was more suitable for coach work. Both versions were powered by the 9.8-litre O.600 engine and four-speed synchromesh gearbox. The Leopard fitted the gap nicely between the lighter Tiger Cub and the heavy-duty Worldmaster and was essentially a Tiger Cub chassis with a more powerful engine. In 1961, Construction and Use regulations were amended, bringing Britain in line with most other European countries and allowing the maximum length of a PSV to be increased to 36 feet.

It was at that year's Scottish Motor Show that Leyland unveiled its range of longer Leopards. Offered with synchromesh or pneumocyclic (semi-automatic) gearboxes, the chassis designation was changed to PSU3, and while the L1 and L2 remained available, they were later modified to bring them in line with the PSU3 range, and so were designated PSU4. From 1966 the Leopard became a true heavyweight chassis when the larger 11.3-litre O.680 engine was made available in vehicles fitted with the pneumocyclic gearbox. While most operators elected to take the larger engine configuration, the Scottish Bus Group (SBG) continued to take the synchromesh gearbox Leopard with the O.600 engine until it was discontinued in 1973.

Construction and Use regulations were relaxed again in 1967, this time allowing vehicles to be built to a maximum length of 39 feet, and in 1970 the PSU5 was introduced, initially only available with the pneumocyclic gearbox (which now also included a ten-speed splitter version). It was not until the end of AEC Reliance production in 1979 that the PSU5 was available with a manual gearbox, when pressure from operators loyal to the Reliance persuaded Leyland to introduce a ZF gearbox option to the PSU3 and PSU5. Throughout its lifespan, the Leopard was subject to Leyland's programme of continuous improvement, particularly in relation to driver and vehicle safety. Many improvements and alterations to the Leopard chassis were made, mostly in connection with the braking system, and in 1982, with the TL11-powered Tiger already launched, the Leopard received a rationalised version of the O.680 which shared numerous TL11 components. Despite these improvements, new European legislations on engine noise, emissions and braking regulations due to be introduced in April 1983 spelled the end for the Leopard, and the last chassis for the UK market were constructed in 1982, with a deadline for the vehicles to be completed by the end of March 1983.

Southend Transport was no stranger to rebodying batches of buses for use in their own fleet, but Weymann-bodied Leopard L1 2717 HJ of 1961 received its new lease of life after it left Southend. In 1981, Horlocks Coaches of Northfleet replaced the Weymann body seen here with a Plaxton Panorama Elite, originally fitted to Bedford VAM JAR 611G. Such was the extent of the rebuild that the little Leopard received age-related registration OKE 791W. (AS)

It is no coincidence that Halifax and Glasgow Corporation's liveries of were so similar. In 1930, Halifax took delivery of an AEC Regent demonstrator which had formerly been with and retained the livery of Glasgow. The Tramways Committee at Halifax were so impressed by the livery they adopted it as their own. Halifax 37 (PJX 37), another L1 with a Weymann body, is seen in Crossfield bus station, Halifax, in 1968. (AS)

Between 1923 and 1969, the mighty Midland Red built its own buses under the BMMO banner. In the early 1960s the need to replace older vehicles was going at a pace quicker than new vehicles could be built, allowing outside manufacturers to enter the fleet. In 1962, the first single-deck Leylands arrived: PSU3 Leopards bodied by Willowbrook or Weymann. By now firmly in the NBC era, Willowbrook-bodied 5209 is seen parked in Stratford-on-Avon. (AS)

One of the few independent operators to become part of the NBC was Venture Transport of Consett, County Durham. Venture was the largest independent bus operator in North East England and in 1970 its entire fleet of eighty-six buses was sold to the Northern General Transport Company. Venture was operated as a separate entity within Northern, hence Alexander-bodied Leopard 236 (9536 PT) receiving full NBC livery but with Venture names. (AS)

New in 1961, Edinburgh Corporation Leopard 101 (YSG 101) was fitted with an experimental three-door Alexander Y-type body. Passengers entered by the double doors at the rear onto a wide platform containing a seated conductor, exit being by the centre and front doors. It seated thirty-three and had room for a further forty standees. In 1968 it was converted to single-door configuration and was painted black and white for use on the airport service. It wasn't withdrawn until 1988, becoming Edinburgh's longest serving bus. (AS)

Another of the three divisional areas of SELNEC was Northern, which encompassed the fleets from Rochdale, Leigh, Ramsbottom, Bury and Bolton, and a vehicle from the last fleet is seen in its home town bus station. Now 6012 in the SELNEC fleet, UWH 322 was a 1963 Leopard L1 fitted with an East Lancs dual-purpose body. (CE)

With their operating territories crossing the Scottish–English border, both Western SMT and Eastern Scottish had depots south of the border. In Carlisle, Western SMT shared a depot with Cumberland Motor Services, and it is from there that 1837 (VCS 391), a 1963 Leopard PSU3 with an Alexander Y-type body, is seen emerging in 1970. (AS)

Todmorden Corporation commenced bus operation in 1907, and in 1931 the LMS took a 50 per cent share in the company, resulting in the formation of the Todmorden Joint Omnibus Committee. In 1971, Todmorden and Halifax JOCs were merged to form Calderdale JOC. Seen in Burnley bus station prior to the merger is Todmorden 37 (573 EYG), a 1963 East Lancs-bodied Leyland L1. (AS)

Ralph Bennett, the forward-thinking general manager of Bolton Corporation, was responsible for modernisation of the fleet. Fitting translucent roof panels to double-deckers to add more light and ordering the first rear-engined double-deckers were among his achievements. Four consecutively registered East Lancs-bodied Leopards were delivered in 1963 – two L2s and two PSU3s. YBN 16, one of the former, is seen in Bolton's central bus station in 1969. (AS)

Caerphilly Urban District Council commenced bus operations in 1920, and continued to do so until the 1972 Local Government Act saw the fleet amalgamated with Bedwas & Machen and Gelligaer to form Rhymney Valley District Council. 14 (ATX 514B), a 1964 Leopard PSU3 with a rather austere-looking Massey body, is seen at Caerphilly's depot in 1972. (AS)

As well as local bus work, Hull-based East Yorkshire Motor Services operated a network of longer-distance express services. Seen wearing EYMS's handsome blue and cream dual-purpose livery is rather elegant Willowbrook-bodied Leopard PSU3 772 (9772 RH), departing Mansfield bus station on the Scarborough to Birmingham service in 1969. (AS)

In 1964, declining passenger numbers saw West Hartlepool Corporation introduce one-person operated buses. Five Leopard L1s with unusual dual-door Strachan bodies were bought to operate the inaugural services, with PEF 23 (every new bus purchased by West Hartlepool had an 'EF' registration) being the last of the batch. In 1967, West Hartlepool was merged with much smaller neighbour Hartlepool Transport to form the County Borough of Hartlepool Transport Department. (AS)

In 1960, Peckham-based Charles. W. Banfield purchased the old established Empire's Best (Webber Bros), who operated a thrice-daily service from London to the Essex coast. In 1965, two Willowbrook-bodied Leopards PSU3s arrived, both in a dedicated livery for the Empire's Best service. Despite looking slightly down at heel, LMD 544C was to see further service with West Wales of Tycroes after withdrawal by Banfield's. (AS)

Pennine of Gargrave was formed in 1925 by brothers Arthur and Vic Simpson and their brother-in-law Jim Windle, choosing the name Pennine as this was the area they intended to serve. The distinctive orange and black livery was adopted when the partners visited the Leyland factory and saw a bus painted in the factory football team's colours of orange with a black stripe. Seen in Lancaster bus station, deep in Ribble's operating territory, is Roe-bodied Leopard L1 LWU 499D. (AS)

Despite being taken over by Midland Red in 1935, Stratford Blue remained a separate entity until 1971. The last vehicle delivered prior to Stratford Blue being fully integrated into the Midland Red fleet was HAC 628D a dual-purpose Marshall-bodied Leopard L2. Seen here in 1988 at Midland Red (West)'s Worcester depot, its subsequent life as a trainee vehicle (you'd have thought it would have known what to do by now...) helped it end up in preservation. (CE)

A little more tuition required, I feel. Looking somewhat battle-scarred is Southend Transport's Leopard GJN 509D. Thankfully its wounds are superficial, affecting only the decorative fibreglass mouldings. The front entrance has been dispensed with to provide accommodation for the instructor, and I wouldn't mind betting that he picked his feet up when this happened! One of the last remaining PD3s and a Daimler Fleetline are also in this 1979 shot. (MH)

Despite a previous attempt by Exeter Corporation to sell the city's bus fleet to Devon General falling at the last hurdle, the formation of the NBC provided the perfect opportunity for the two operations to be amalgamated. Although some Exeter buses remained in corporation colours until as late as 1979, former Exeter Massey-bodied Leopard PSU4 GFJ 603D had received full NBC poppy red. It is seen in Exeter bus station surrounded by vehicles new to both Exeter and Devon General. (MH)

1 October 1976 saw the formation of Isle of Man National Transport Ltd, as a result of the merger between the two previous bus operators on the island, Douglas Corporation and Isle of Man Road Services. Being the larger of the two, the IoMRS livery was chosen for the new fleet, as seen on former IoMRS Willowbrook-bodied Leopard 698 HMN on layover in Douglas bus station. (MH)

United Services of South Yorkshire was a consortium of three companies providing bus services across Doncaster and Wakefield. All buses were painted in a common livery of blue and cream and all used the United Services fleetname. Bingley of Kinsley was one of the three, and Plaxton-bodied Leopard PSU3 AWX 118G, purchased new, is seen picking up in South Elmsall bus station. (RS)

In 1972, the NBC introduced a corporate livery, which (with one or two notable exceptions) was poppy red or leaf green for buses and white for coaches. Vehicles capable of fulfilling dual roles had their bottom half painted in fleet colours with the top half painted white. East Yorkshire were one of the notable exceptions, retaining an attractive shade of blue as seen on dual-purpose Marshall-bodied Leopard PSU3 878 (RKH 878G), in London Victoria coach station waiting to depart for home. (AS)

In 1966, Fishwick's purchased the local coachbuilding concern of W. H. Fowler. Fowler's had previously been responsible for Fishwick's maintenance, and while this arrangement continued, they also built a handful of rather angular bus bodies for their new parent company. One of three PSU4 Leopards to receive Fowler bodywork was 27 (BTD 780J), seen when about to leave Preston bus station in 1973. (AS)

The Carmarthenshire village of Tycroes could once boast two large independent bus operators: Rees & Williams and West Wales. It was also served by South Wales Transport, and such was the working relationship between West Wales and SWT that SWT vehicles were outstationed in West Wales' depot and SWT carried out vehicle painting for West Wales. The relationship would come full circle in the 1990s when West Wales was sold to SWT. Willowbrook-bodied MBX 86H is one of several Leopard buses bought new. (MH)

For nearly seventy years, W. Gash & Sons of Newark provided local bus services across Nottinghamshire and Lincolnshire using both double- and single-deck buses, and for almost half its existence only brand-new vehicles were purchased. Following deregulation, the company grew in size, but in 1989 the Gash family decided to sell. The company passed to the Yorkshire Traction Group and was integrated into the Lincolnshire Road Car fleet. Plaxtons were the favoured body, as shown on brand-new PSU3 Leopard L08 (GNN 348J). (AS)

The Leopard was a good export model for Leyland, and sold particularly well in Australia, including numerous examples for St Ives Bus Service of Pymble, a suburb of Sydney, NSW. Established by Arthur Gillott in 1935, the firm began with two small tip trucks, but by the 1990s had grown to a fleet in excess of eighty vehicles ranging from heavy haulage prime movers to service buses. Seen at the depot in St Ives, Custom Coaches Manufacturing Company (CCMC)-bodied Leopard MO.5420 was new in 1972 and stayed with St Ives until 1996. (Norman Chambers)

Staying in Australia, Frankston Passenger Services operated a dozen or so vehicles on stage routes around the Melbourne suburb of Frankston until being absorbed into Peninsula Bus Lines in 2002. New in 1974, LHU 535 was an Ansair-bodied Leopard, Ansair being formed in 1945 to manufacture bodies for Ansett Pioneer coaches as well as aircraft components for Ansett Airways. (Geoff Foster)

With the closure of the BMMO factory and its integration into the NBC, Midland Red's vehicle purchases fell in line with its fellow NBC subsidiaries. Marshall-bodied PSU3 Leopards PHA 334/5M were part of the fifty-strong S28 class delivered between 1974 and 1975. They are seen at Worcester, where they were used on Motorway Express services X43 and X44. (AS)

It is purely coincidental that this image is also of an S28 class Midland Red Leopard, as it was the operator rather than the vehicle I selected it for. Black Prince of Morley near Leeds (named after Edward, the Black Prince, a statue of whom stands in the centre of Leeds) was formed in 1969 by Brian Crowther. When taken over by FirstGroup in 2005 it had grown to operate over forty vehicles and was the last family owned independent bus operator in Leeds. GOH 361N came to Black Prince from Irvine of Law, and is seen outside the Wray's Buildings in Vicar Lane, Leeds. (RS)

Seen parked in Pond Street bus station, Sheffield, is Richardson of Sheffield's dual-door Plaxton-bodied PSU3 Leopard JDK 922P, new to Lancashire United Transport. Formed in 1976, Richardson's took advantage of deregulation to build up a network of services in and around Sheffield before selling out to South Yorkshire Transport, Mr Richardson then moving south to form Richardson's of Midhurst. (RS)

Duple used the Dominant name for both bus and coach bodies throughout the 1970s and early 1980s despite there being no real family resemblance between the two body styles. The Dominant bus first appeared in 1975 and remained in production until replaced by the 300 series over ten years later. Graham's of Paisley used a number of Dominant bus-bodied Leopards, including S8 (MUS 151P), which was bought new in 1976 and is seen at the company's depot with the Ciba-Geigy pigment plant as a backdrop. (AS)

Paisley's neighbouring town of Renfrew was home to Paton Bros, whose fleet of cream and blue buses, most of which were bought new, were taken over by Western SMT in 1979. Gilmour Street Paisley sees Willowbrook-bodied Leopard NGE 614P in front of one of Western SMT's earliest rear-engined double-deckers, an Alexander-bodied Daimler Fleetline. MH recollects that the driver drove away either unaware, or not bothered, that his offside engine flap was ajar. (MH)

For many years, the number of UK buses exported for further service in Malta made it a Mecca for enthusiasts hankering for the nostalgic days of 'proper' buses, although you never knew if what you were travelling on was what it actually said on the box. Looking remarkably restrained for a Maltese bus, with just a polished front panel added to its brightwork, is Plaxton Derwent-bodied PSU4 Leopard EBY-543, new to West Yorkshire PTE in 1976 as LUG 524P. (RJ)

Ventura Bus Lines in Melbourne had a long tradition of purchasing Leylands from the early 1960s to the late 1980s, with many Royal Tiger Cubs, Leopards and Tigers featuring on everyday route work. They also operated Leopards and a Panther bodied as coaches. IKK 059, a 1975 Ansair-bodied Leopard, is seen when new at South Oakleigh depot. (Geoff Foster)

The Londonderry & Lough Swilly Railway was incorporated in 1853 and by the end of the nineteenth century had established a network of narrow-gauge lines. In 1929, buses entered the fleet, their numbers increasing as the rail network shrank. In 1971, buying policy changed to sourcing used buses and coaches from UK operators, and the first of 266 Leopards entered service. In 2014, after 161 years of service, Lough Swilly ceased trading, the oldest transport company in the world passing into history. Alexander-bodied 423 (80 DL 729), formerly GCS 56V, was new to Western Scottish. (MH)

Safeguard of Guildford operated a number of Duple Dominant buses, mostly on Leopard chassis. OPC 26R is seen in Guildford bus station in the company of similarly bodied Leyland Tiger C164 SPB. It's pleasing to see that bus usage was good enough to require a relief which itself has a healthy load. Happily, both operator and bus are still with us, OPC having been lovingly preserved, and Safeguard celebrating their ninety-fifth anniversary in 2019. (MH)

In 1918, Mrs Alice Poole lost both her husband and eldest son in a mining disaster, and in 1924 founded Poole & Sons, using the compensation from the disaster fund. The company later became Poole's Coachways Ltd and operated until 1987, providing regular services between Audley and Newcastle-under-Lyme. Willowbrook were the favoured bodybuilders; however, XFA 967S was fitted with a Marshall Camair body due to industrial unrest at Willowbrook. (RS)

After deregulation, well-known coach tour operator Shearings set up a bus operation, initially based in the north-west of England. Through acquisitions, the operating area expanded before the whole of the bus operation was sold. Timeline, the new operator, retained Shearings colours, as can be seen on Alexander T-type-bodied Leopard GLS 275S entering Wolverhampton bus station. Rather a globetrotting bus, it was new in 1978 to Alexander (Midland), passing to Cumberland and then Blue Bus of Horwich before ending up with Southern National. (RS)

The Alexander Y type was in production for over twenty years, and was built on most chassis types available in Britain during that time. The vast majority were built on Leopards, mostly for the Scottish Bus Group. This post-privatisation shot of Lovers Lane garage in Thurso sees two former Highland Scottish Y types now owned by Highland Country sandwiching a Plaxton Supreme-bodied Volvo B58. Seemingly identical, the rear vehicle has the long panoramic window option. (MH)

Northern & Western Bus Lines of Gladesville, New South Wales, operated this attractive step-decked Leopard, bodied by PMC (Pressed Metal Corporation NSW, a division of JRA – Jaguar Rover Australia). MO.474, pictured departing Chatswood station, was one of fourteen purchased in 1980. The vertical exhaust at the offside rear was NSW law at the time for diesel-engined vehicles over a certain weight so monitoring of exhaust emissions could be easily undertaken in traffic. (Norman Chambers)

While Duple's Dominant bus looked nothing like its coaching counterpart, Plaxton's Bustler had a strong family resemblance to the Supreme range it ran alongside, as seen on the sixty-four-seat OWG 368X, delivered new to Premier (Harold Wilson) of Stainforth. Introduced in 1980, all Bustlers were delivered to independent operators, and while it didn't sell in huge numbers, it announced Plaxton's re-entry into the bus market after a gap of five years, its predecessor the Derwent having been discontinued in 1977. (RS)

The Warrior, a rather angular Leyland Lynx lookalike, was Willowbrook's final crack at the UK bus market. All but one were rebodies on older chassis, in some cases replacing earlier Willowbrook 008 'Spacecar' coach bodies, as was the case with GIB 5970, previously XCW 153R, and new to National Travel (West). After rebodying it was delivered to Safeway Services of South Petherton, who for exactly eighty years to the month operated a network of services across south Somerset. (MH)

The Panther

By the early 1960s, manufacturers were designing rear-engined single-deck chassis suitable for both bus and coach work, and at the 1964 Earls Court Motor Show, Leyland launched the Panther. While only offered with an 18-foot 6-inch wheelbase, two separate versions were available: the PSUR1.1 for bus work and the PSUR1.2, which was intended mainly for coaching activities. In order to obtain a degree of commonality it was decided to use the same chassis frames for both the Panther and for AEC's new rear-engined bus, the Swift. Unlike the Swift, the Panther had a front-mounted radiator, helping to alleviate the overheating issues that dogged the Southall product. However, it was with the Leopard that the Panther shared a closer relationship as they featured the same pneumocyclic gearbox and Leyland O.600 engine, both mounted behind the rear axle. The Panther bus had a low chassis from the front of the vehicle, which then stepped up over the engine and gearbox at a point just ahead of the rear axle. This allowed bodybuilders to create a body offering wide one-step entry and exit doors with a flat floor for most of the vehicle.

It was unfortunate for the Panther, with its advance technical specification, that it had the Leopard as its 'zoo-mate'. Operators were still getting used to a large volume of legislation which had been introduced in the last decade, and they appeared to be rather conservative when it came to vehicle buying, preferring to stick to the tried and tested. The final Panthers were built in 1972, and while its production run was probably one of the shortest of the post-war Leyland models, the practical experience it gave Leyland was to prove invaluable when the next generation of rear-engined single-deck vehicles was introduced later that same year.

At the start of the 1970s, with rising costs and staff shortages, one-person operation became more of a necessity. Wilts & Dorset's problem was a large fleet of front-engined double-deckers and not enough suitable single-deckers. The answer was for thirty-three relatively new Panthers to transfer from Maidstone & District. Reliable sources say that M&D got the better end of the deal when the Panthers departed west. Willowbrook-bodied 687 (JKK 198E) is seen surrounded by some beautiful Bristols in Basingstoke bus station. (AS)

With the Panther's engine mounted in-line, the low-floor bus version required the chassis to step upwards towards the rear. Most bodybuilders stepped the window line to match, as can be seen on Cleveland Transit's Park Royal-bodied S328 (VUP 906F), new to Stockton and seen in Stockton High Street complete with informative destination blind. (AS)

Formed in 1922 to operate a bus service around Wakefield and Castleford, by the mid-1950s West Riding was the largest private bus company in Britain. Well known for their involvement in the ill-fated Guy Wulfrunian project (operating 132 out of the 137 vehicles built), they also took fifty Panthers. New in 1968, Roe-bodied 163 (LHL 163F) is seen at Belle Isle garage near Wakefield. (AS)

Lincoln Corporation also followed the trend for introducing OPO buses and, starting in 1967, took twenty-five Roe-bodied Panthers delivered over four batches. The Roe body featured a straight waist rail as seen on 44 (EVL 552E) and 55 (KVL 55H), a bus I remember when it passed to Webber's of Blisland, Cornwall. Both are parked in Oxford Street, Lincoln, with Central station in the background. (RS)

This really emphasises how low the Panther was, with the height from the floor to the top of the wheel arch almost the same as the top of the wheel arch to the cant rail. The raised rear seating to clear the engine can clearly be seen through the windows of Fishwick's 1 (JTJ 667F), a Park Royal-bodied Panther originally built as a demonstrator and seen in Preston's old Fox Street bus station. (AS)

Back when London Victoria coach station was a myriad of colours rather than the white of today's National Express coaches, East Yorkshire's dual-purpose Marshall-bodied Panther 848 (MAT 848F) arrives in the departure side, waiting for its allocated stand. East Yorkshire was the only operator to take Panthers in bus, dual-purpose and full coach guise. (AS)

Liverpool Corporation took the largest number of Panthers for the UK market, with 110, all fitted with MCW bodies. By the time this picture of 1010 (FKF 889F) was taken in Southport, Liverpool had become part of Merseyside PTE. Whereas the body on Fishwick's Panther looked too small for the chassis, the MCW body appears too big, the front wheels looking lost inside the body. (AS)

Even though Strachan bodied nearly 100 Panthers, they were only delivered to two operators, Sunderland and Maidstone & District. From the latter fleet is 3134 (LKT 134F), seen pulling out of Pevensey Road bus station, Eastbourne, en route to Uckfield, leaving behind a Southdown Leopard heading in the same direction. There is such wonderful signage on the buildings; you can just imagine Captain Mainwaring with his copy of the *Eastbourne Gazette* and *Herald Chronicle*. (AS)

Preston's Panthers were bodied by MCW, Seddon and Marshall and included the last Panther delivered to a UK operator. The five MCW-bodied examples arrived first and featured the stepped waist rail, which unfortunately did nothing to help the rather haphazard application of Preston's livery, as seen on 202 (HCK 202G). In 1971, five further Panthers arrived, second-hand examples originating with Stratford Blue. (AS)

Southport Corporation also had MCW-bodied Panthers, including 67 (JWM 67F). However, all had their windows level with the cant rail and flowing side mouldings, making for an altogether more pleasant-looking bus. Southport's attractive red and cream livery was to disappear when the fleet was incorporated into Merseyside PTE. (AS)

Neepsend of Sheffield, sister company to 'other side of the Pennines' East Lancs of Blackburn, bodied ten Panthers for Chesterfield, all based on an East Lancs design. Differing-sized numbers in the destination box, as well as the broken blind, do nothing to improve the rather down-at-heel-looking front end on 86 (SRB 86F).

The twelve Roe-bodied Panthers delivered to Kingston upon Hull in 1965 were the first 30-foot single-deckers for the company and the longest buses ever delivered to them. 73 (CRH 173C) is seen in 1971 in Lombard St Central garage, now demolished as part of the St Stephen's shopping development. (CE)

On a sunny spring day in the early 1980s, two Panthers rest between duties in the Derbyshire market town of Bakewell. Both were owned by the Silver Service group, with the ex-Liverpool Corporation bus at the front wearing the red Hulley's of Baslow livery. A good picture to compare the two differing body styles, straight through ex-Lancaster East Lancs-bodied LTC 109F at the rear with the stepped waist rail ex-Liverpool bus bodied by MCW. (MH)

In 1974 Grenda's bus service of Dandenong bought a batch of Panthers and Panther Cubs imported from the UK via Wollongong dealer Jimmy Hill. 35 (LUN 264) was a Metro-Cammell-bodied Panther, new in 1967 as Manchester Corporation 48 (GND 93E). (Geoff Foster)

Grenda also bought six new Denning-bodied Panthers in 1969 for use on their trunk service along the Princes Highway from Dandenong to Chadstone. 95 (KLU 554) is seen in the experimental red and white livery, tried around 1980. (Geoff Foster)

In 1969, Bradford Corporation took delivery of ten rear-engine single-deckers as an evaluation exercise, split equally between the Panther and AEC Swift. When WYPTE was formed, the Panthers were transferred to Halifax, where 509 (NAK 509H) is seen still wearing full Bradford livery. All were withdrawn from service shortly afterwards following a fatal accident where a blind spot caused by the thickness of the offside corner pillar was cited as the contributory factor. Subsequently, a small window was cut into each pillar and the buses were sold to Chesterfield for further service. (RS)

The last single-deck buses purchased by Lytham Corporation before becoming Fylde Borough were three Northern Counties-bodied Panthers. At the end of the 1960s, two were hired to Stonier's of Goldenhill, where TTF 745H is seen at the rear of Stonier's depot. They were reported to have been reliable, but somewhat lethargic, and in the hands of a less-skilled driver wouldn't climb Stonebank Road in Kidsgrove. (MH)

The Burnley, Colne & Nelson Joint Transport Committee was established in 1933 to merge the three town's transport operations. The 1972 Local Government Act saw Colne and Nelson amalgamated to form Pendle, creating the Burnley & Pendle JTC. Burnley bus station sees Northern Counties-bodied Panther 75 (HHG 75F) freshly repainted in Burnley & Pendle livery, while similarly bodied Bristol RE LHG 387H behind retains BC&N livery. (AS)

Northern General ordered twenty-three Marshall Camair-bodied Panthers, including five for standalone subsidiaries Tyneside Omnibus Company and Tynemouth & District. Seen in Sunderland bus station is 2338 (GCN 838G), complete with NBC fleetnames but still painted in Northern's slightly darker red, and surprisingly for a Northern bus it's not telling you to 'Shop at Binns'. (RS)

Much like almost every bus in the Northern General fleet implored you to 'Shop at Binns', Devon General buses always seemed to carry yellow adverts telling you that you just had to visit Kent's Cavern or Babbacombe Model Village. Marshall-bodied Panther MFJ 388G was one of the last buses delivered to Exeter Corporation before the fleet was merged into Devon General. Exeter used letters rather than numbers for their city services, hence MFJ being unable to display a number for its trip to Axminster. (RS)

Winchester-based 'municipalesque' independent King Alfred Motor Services had a rather eclectic vehicle-buying policy towards the end of its existence, and was one of only two UK independents to purchase new Panther buses. UOU 418H was one of three Plaxton Derwent-bodied examples delivered in 1970, and is seen in a location synonymous with KAMS: The Broadway in Winchester. (AS)

When the metropolitan county of Greater Manchester was created on 1 April 1974, SELNEC became Greater Manchester Transport and increased both its fleet size and operating area by taking over Wigan Corporation's buses. Freshly painted and complete with the new GMT logo is former Wigan Northern Counties-bodied Panther 1690 (HJP 960H), seen in its home town in 1975. (AS)

While thirteen might be unlucky for some, Eastbourne certainly didn't feel unlucky with their thirteen East Lancs-bodied Panthers, as all had long lives on the south coast. 9 (HHC 909J) stands adjacent to Eastbourne Pier in 1980, while Plaxton Supreme-bodied Bedford YMT YPB 820T of Blue Saloon of Guildford loads it's private hire party. I have looked at countless pictures of Eastbourne's Panthers, and in none of them is the metal plate below the windscreen actually being used for anything! (MH)

Growing up in Cornwall in the 1980s was great fun: the weather, the views, the beaches and the buses – vehicles that most of the country had long since dispensed with. North Cornwall Cars of Langdon Cross was an operator whose fleet always seemed to be on its last legs. They ran two of these Marshall Camair-bodied Panthers as well as an ex-Lincoln example. AUE 311/2J were from a batch of five delivered to Stratford Blue just as Midland Red took full control, and unwanted by Midland Red they were bought by Preston. I've just noticed the registration on the Peugeot 504: another private plate to add to my collection. (MH)

Tyneside PTE, the predecessor to Tyne & Wear PTE, not only inherited Panthers from Newcastle and Sunderland, but also took delivery of five with dual-purpose Alexander W-type bodies. 23 (KBB 523L) is seen in Haymarket, Newcastle. The driver is either not too happy about having his photo taken or he's just noticed the engine cover is open. (AS)

Let's finish the Panther section with a superb shot of a bygone era. With its gleaming green and cream livery with brightwork polished and a smartly uniformed driver complete with white topped cap, Maidstone & District's Strachan-bodied LKT 124F turns off Susans Road into the old Cavendish Place coach station in Eastbourne. (AS)

The Panther Cub

The PSUC Panther Cub was essentially the Panther's smaller sibling. Leyland had identified Manchester Corporation as a potential launch customer for the Panther. However, Manchester wanted a 10-metre-long rear-engined single-decker, and told Leyland that if wouldn't build such a vehicle then they would look to an alternative chassis manufacturer. Launched in 1964, the Panther Cub's chassis was similar to the Panther's (upswept to the rear) but about 2 feet shorter, and most major components apart from the engine and gearbox were standard Panther components. Construction and Use regulations on maximum rear overhang precluded the use of the O.600 engine used in the Panther, so the O.400 engine as used in the Tiger Cub was used, along with the same pneumocyclic gearbox.

Manchester kept to its word and ordered twenty Panther Cubs. However, they were woefully underpowered to the extent that ten of the twenty had turbochargers fitted, designed to give more torque at lower engine speeds rather than increase horsepower, but the turbocharged engines suffered from blown head gaskets and in the end all turbochargers were removed.

As well as its lack of power, the Panther Cub's future wasn't helped by the 1965 share exchange between the Department of Transport and Leyland, which saw Leyland take a 25 per cent stake in Bristol Commercial Vehicles. This removed the previous sales restrictions on Bristol buses being sold on the open market, and as the highly successful Bristol RE was available in 10-metre form and could be fitted with higher output Leyland and Gardner engines, the writing was on the wall for the Panther Cub. Production ceased in 1968, with a total of ninety-four built, all for English and Welsh operators, and all bodied as buses.

Despite the Panther Cub being produced to satisfy Manchester Corporation, they had rather short service lives there. ANF 161B, one of the initial duo delivered in 1964, soon passed to Cooper Bros of South Kirby, part of the United Services co-operative. It may have been unloved in Manchester but gave sterling service at Cooper's, even retaining its Manchester destination blind in the nearside aperture for all its time with Cooper's. (AS)

It is reputed that Mr Fred Varney founded Golden Miller after a winning bet on the horse with the same name which won the Cheltenham Gold Cup and the Grand National in 1934. Who knows if he backed another winner when he bought Park Royal-bodied Panther Cub BND 868C from Manchester! The bus is seen waiting time at Feltham station in 1973. (AS)

Park Royal-bodied Panther Cub GUP 502C was new in 1965 to Stockton Corporation, which had originally become part of Teesside Municipal Transport, Teesside then becoming Cleveland Transit. Seen in 1974 in Stockton depot wearing Cleveland's green and jasmine livery, visible in the background is at least one vehicle still wearing the old Teesside turquoise. (RS)

Two of the three fleets which merged to form Teesside operated Panther Cubs. Now S309 in the Cleveland Transit fleet, Northern Counties-bodied DXG 401D was new in 1966 to Middlesbrough Corporation, and is seen leaving Middlesbrough's Parliament Road garage with a rather intriguing destination. (RS)

Strachan-bodied 92 (YTB 771D) was originally a Leyland demonstrator and was sent to Eastbourne to provide transport for delegates going to the 1967 Municipal Passenger Transport Association conference. Once its duties had been completed, it was purchased by Eastbourne and is seen here being chased down Grove Road by a Triumph Herald in 1968. (AS)

The only independent operator to purchase Panther Cubs from new was Thomas of Port Talbot, who took three Strachan-bodied examples in 1966. They lasted in service long enough not only for the Thomas takeover by South Wales Transport, but also for the introduction of NBC corporate livery. 505 (HTG 181D) is seen in Port Talbot garage in 1975. (AS)

Ashton bus station in July 1969, a month after I was born there (Ashton that is, not the bus station; however the ambulance did break down en route so who knows what could have happened!) sees Ashton-under-Lyne Corporation 56 (CTC 356E), a 1967 East Lancs-bodied Panther Cub. Lurking in the background is Manchester Corporation Leyland PD2 3543 (UNB 543). (AS)

Portsmouth Corporation took the largest number of Panthers Cubs, with twenty-six being delivered in two batches in 1967. Despite being delivered over two differing registration suffixes, all had consecutive GTP registration numbers. The first twelve were bodied by Marshall, with the remainder, including GTP 165F, being bodied by MCW. Withdrawals commenced in 1977, with the last ones leaving the fleet by 1980. (AS)

I make no apologies for including a black and white picture as I've only driven one Panther Cub and it was this one. KED 546F was one of four East Lancs-bodied examples delivered to Warrington in 1967. Not knowing the Panther Cub's chequered history when I drove it, I had no preconceived ideas as to its performance, and remember it as a lovely little motor, plodding happily along the motorway at 50 mph (we took it trouble free from Bristol to Manchester and back). There can't be many chassis that can boast almost 5 per cent of their total production in preservation, but the Panther Cub can, as four out of the ninety four built are still alive. (TW)

Above and below: Even though Wigan Corporation came under control of Greater Manchester Transport in 1974 and Ashton having been part of GMT's predecessor, SELNEC, from 1969, the combined GMT Panther Cub fleet was still less than that of Portsmouth. Wigan's two Panther Cubs, DJP 468E and EEK 1F, both had locally built Massey bodies, and despite having different suffixes were both delivered in August 1967. DJP 468E was the first ex-Wigan bus to be painted in GMT orange and white (compare how much its orange has faded with the freshly repainted double-decker in the garage). DJP was exported to Malta, repatriated in the early 2000s and is currently undergoing long term restoration in its home town. (CE/RS)

East Yorkshire took sixteen Panther Cubs in 1968, all with full-height Marshall bodies. All managed a full ten to twelve years' service, and received the short-lived blue and white version of NBC corporate livery applied to EYMS vehicles. Judging by the smile on his face, the driver of 841 (PKH 841G) certainly didn't mind what he was driving as he travels down Pavement in York, past what is now the start of the Merchants' Quarter in Fossgate. (RS)

Until the early 1970s, Brighton Corporation and Brighton, Hove & District shared the same red and cream livery, the result of an operating agreement. The last corporation vehicles delivered carrying it were the seven Panther Cubs delivered in 1968. With a nasty dent in its front panel, Marshal-bodied 41 (NUF 141G), the penultimate Panther Cub to be built, is followed by Weymann-bodied Leyland PD2 24 (24 ACD) from the Brighton Corporation fleet and an unidentified Southdown 'Queen Mary'. Despite the PD2 being five years older than the Panther Cub, it outlasted it by a number of years, all the Panthers being withdrawn by 1975. (AS)

With the formation of the NBC, Southdown took over the operations of Brighton, Hove & District, and, wanting to establish its own identity, Brighton Corporation repainted its fleet light blue and white. Looking so much less impressive in its new colours, Strachan-bodied 37 (NUF 137G) turns out of Lower Rock Gardens in 1972. (AS)

The National

As a book showcasing the Leyland National has already been written by two of my fellow Amberley authors, I have deliberately kept this chapter short so as to not detract from that excellent publication. As has been mentioned in earlier chapters, the formation of British Leyland brought numerous previously competing models together under one umbrella, and so some form of standardisation was needed. The largest bus operator in the UK at the time was the National Bus Company, and the two nationalised industries worked together to produce a bus which would allow Leyland to replace all the different modes in its catalogue, leading to standardisation for the operators.

The National was built at a new factory in Workington, Cumbria, and was integrally constructed using a riveting procedure that made panel replacement much easier and quicker than before. Many components were interchangeable, including the sophisticated heating system which utilised a roof-mounted pod fitted to the rear of the bus, and the driving cab was built to be as ergonomically friendly as possible. The National was fitted with the fixed-head 8.3-litre turbocharged Leyland 510 engine, which was to prove unpopular with operators due to poor fuel consumption and heavy smoking if not maintained correctly. It was available in three lengths: 10.3 and 11.3 metres for the UK market, and 10.9 metres for the Australian market, where axle weight limits precluded the use of the longer bus. As the National was aimed primarily at NBC subsidiaries, early vehicles were only offered in either red or green and only in dual-door layout; however, pressure from operators, primarily London Transport, saw the number of base colours extended.

A simplified version of the National known as the B Series was brought out in 1978. Offered only in single-door and 10.3-metre length, with a simplified heating system which removed the need for the roof mounted pod and a revised interior with minimal lighting, it was aimed at rural rather than urban operations, primarily to replace the Bristol LH. Both the standard and B Series Nationals were replaced in 1979 with the introduction of the National 2. Outwardly similar apart from the bulbous front end which now housed the front-mounted radiator and a restyled rear end, the main difference with the National 2 was the choice of engines. When launched, the National 2 was fitted with the O.680, and later with the TL11. From 1982, Gardner engines were also available following a successful court action brought by Gardner against Leyland's refusal to offer their engines in the National 2.

Some operators experimented with different engine options or rebuilt the vehicles themselves. However, some took things to another level. In the early 1990s, London & Country and East Lancs, both part of the Drawlane Group, began a joint venture to give mid-life Nationals a full rebuild. The engineering work, which involved replacing everything but the framing and axles, was undertaken by London & Country at Reigate before the chassis were sent north to East Lancs for replacement bodywork. This project, known as the National Greenway, was moderately successful, operators finding that the National's integral structure was generally sound, and rebuilding was a more cost-effective option than buying new vehicles.

The first National, ERM 35K was delivered in 1972 to Cumberland Motor Services, the Workington factory's local NBC subsidiary, and over 7,000 vehicles were built before C49 OCM, the last National 2, was delivered to Halton Transport in 1985.

One of the first Nationals to be delivered is seen in Wrexham, having just arrived from the factory. Crosville's SNL805 (WFM 805L) was an 11.3-metre version and sports a full set of Leyland badges across the front. With the introduction of the NBC livery, buses and coaches generally lost any manufacturers badging to make room for corporate logos. (AS)

Plymouth Corporation were such staunch Leyland users that between 1946 and 1983 only six non-Leylands entered the fleet. It was also completely double-deck, so it came as a surprise when in July 1972 Plymouth received the thirteenth production National. A month later delivery of a further fifty-nine commenced, and the first of these was 17 (SCO 417L), seen in Royal Parade, Plymouth. (AS)

As soon as Leyland offered the National in single-door form, London Country ordered forty-seven for use on Green Line routes. The current Green Line fleet consisted of RFs (old), Reliances and Swifts (unreliable), and Routemasters (costly, needing two crew members). Unfortunately for the passengers who were used to coach-style seats, the Nationals had bog-standard bus seats. LNC47 (NPD 147L) is seen in Piccadilly Circus while working a 711 from High Wycombe to Reigate. (AS)

Four earlier members of the NPD batch of Nationals were hired by Nottingham prior to delivery to London Country to operate an experimental free bus service in Nottingham's central shopping area. In 1973 the service was extended to cover a wider part of the central area and sixteen dual-door Nationals were ordered, split equally between 10.3-metre and 11.3-metre versions. From the shorter batch, 726 (GAU 726L) is seen operating service 77 in Mount Street. (AS)

Under the 1972 Local Government Act, Pontypridd UDC became Taff Ely Borough Council. The company had a huge disparity between peak and non-peak vehicle requirement, at one time needing forty-six buses in the evening but only fifteen during the day. Following deregulation it was unable to survive competition from National Welsh, who bought the company in 1988. The first Leyland didn't enter the fleet until 1973. This was 14 (NTX 326L), a forty-four-seat 10.3-metre National seen at Glyntaff, Pontypridd, when a year old. (AS)

'Let's tek the PMT up 'Anley duck.' The city of Stoke-on-Trent is actually a conurbation of six towns, with Hanley as its commercial centre. Just out of sight to the rear of National XEH 249M within the confines of the PMT building at Hanley bus station was my old office, where many an hour was spent wondering what I should next order from the staff canteen. Sadly the old bus station (and its bacon sandwiches) is no more, development of the town centre dictating it be replaced with something more 'suitable' for the twenty-first century. (AS)

Aberdeen Corporation's bus operations were transferred to Grampian Regional Transport in 1975, and a year later twenty Nationals were delivered, including 71 (KSO 71P). Problems with overheating saw them have relatively short lives in Scotland. It is therefore surprising that three were exported to Rockhampton City Council, Queensland, Australia, where they lasted longer than they did in the UK. (AS)

The Melbourne & Metropolitan Tramways Board (MMTB) was a government-owned authority responsible for the inner suburban transport network in Melbourne between 1919 and 1983. Unlike other Australian cities which replaced trams with buses, Melbourne retained its tram network because its wide, geometrically patterned streets made the use of trams more practical than many other cities. Its bus fleet consisted of twenty-five AEC Regal IVs delivered in 1956 and thirty Nationals delivered twenty years later. 817 (IAC.817) is seen at Heidelberg station terminus. (Geoff Foster)

LS1 (TGY 101M) was London Transport's first National, one of six delivered in 1973 to run alongside six Metro-Scanias as an evaluation exercise for its next generation of single-deckers. The National won the day and over 500 more were delivered. LS1 is seen in Clapton Pond passing an AC Thundersley Invacar. Useless trivia alert: in March 2003 the government deemed the Invacar to be unsafe and ordered all remaining examples be destroyed, with over fifty cars a week being crushed. (AS)

London Transport's Mk 1 Nationals only seated thirty-six, allowing plenty of room for standees. LS53 (KJD 553P) from the 1976 delivery is seen leaving Hatton Cross Interchange on a 203 Hounslow–Staines service shortly after delivery, being followed by an SMS class AEC Swift, whose withdrawals were hastened by the delivery of the Nationals. (AS)

The National was a pretty versatile vehicle, with some being built as emergency support vehicles or jumbo ambulances. A name long since gone from the high street is the Midland Bank, but in 1975 they purchased JHV 611N brand new and had it kitted out as a mobile bank for use around rural North Yorkshire. It is seen here in Whitby with Captain Cook keeping an eye on things in the background. (RS)

Caernarfon's Town Square bus station, with the imposing castle towering over it, must have been one of Britain's most attractive locations for such a facility. Now operating with KMP of Llanberis, HFM 185N hadn't travelled far from its original owner, being new to Crosville as fleet number ENL929. (MH)

Sticking with the castle theme, with the spectacular backdrop of Dover Marina and the Old Customs House, an unidentified National of East Kent tackles the long climb up Castle Hill in Dover en route to Deal. The short pod and unrelieved red livery put the National as one of the last nine delivered to East Kent. (MH)

Whether the GB in the registration was a coincidence or deliberate is not known, but West Nederland 3113 (20-67-GB) was one of twenty-five Nationals exported in 1975 for trials with various Dutch operators. In 1976, CAB of Utrecht fitted the distinctive six-piece windscreen to help eliminate glare. They were found to require a lot of maintenance and prone to slipping due their small wheels so no more were imported. It is seen in the Hague bus station, which is above the tram station, which itself is over the railway terminus. (CE)

In 1954, Melbourne-Brighton Bus Lines was formed by the merger of a number of operators who ran from Gardenvale and Middle Brighton into Melbourne. A depot was built in Brighton for the twenty-four-vehicle fleet, operations continuing until 1985 when the services were sold to the Metropolitan Transit Authority. IKW.097 was one of two Nationals delivered in 1976, and is seen passing Melbourne's Flinders Street station, one of Melbourne's most recognisable landmarks. Built in 1909, it is listed on the Victorian Heritage Register. (LJ)

Introduced in 1978, the B Series National was only available in 10.3-metre length, and featured underseat heating and minimal lighting. Alexander (Midlands) first Nationals included ten B Series including OLS 807T. Now operating for Cumberland Motor Services, it is seen in East Street, Carlisle, with the east tower of the Citadel in the background, and surrounded by such icons of the 1980s as a Ford Cargo, Wimpy bar and, joy of joys, an Austin Maestro. (MH)

While independent operators were not at the front of the queue to buy new Nationals, a number of Scottish operators soon made it their standard bus. McGill of Barrhead purchased their first one in 1978 and took a further fourteen, including one of the last National 2s to be built. The first arrival was XYS 596S, seen here at McGill's depot with an eclectic mix of sister ships. Alexander-bodied Daimler Fleetline XHS 924H is sandwiched between Duple-bodied Guy Arab GVD 47 and what at first glance appears to be a Volvo F88, but is actually an Albion Chieftain fitted with an F88 cab. (MH)

National 2 EDT 205V was delivered to Yorkshire Traction in January 1980 and painted in traditional Mexborough and Swinton livery, that company having merged with Yorkshire Traction eleven years to the month earlier. SYPTE buses and Park Hill estate in the background can only mean it's in Sheffield. Note the use of the pay as you enter panel for advertising. (CE)

Not strictly a National, the Leyland-DAB bendibus was a collaboration between Leyland and Dansk Automobil Byggeri of Denmark (Leyland being the majority shareholder in DAB). Only two UK operators ordered them: SYPTE (five in 1979 and thirteen in 1986) and British Airways. The SYPTE ones were assembled at Workington, the BA ones at the Charles H. Roe plant at Crossgates in Leeds. They were used initially on airside transfers at Heathrow, but RLN 237W had migrated north and is seen in Manchester Piccadilly bus station. They seated forty-five with room for a further 100 standees and had five doors, three on the nearside and two on the offside. (RS)

The National 2 was available with the heating system in the traditional roof mounted pod or with a floor-mounted system as per the B Series. Seen in the lovely Derbyshire town of Bakewell is RRA 222X, new in 1981 to Trent, but when photographed had moved not too far down the road to join the fleet of Hulley's of Baslow. (RS)

In 1986 Athelstan Coaches of Malmesbury passed into new ownership, and the trading name of Overland & County was adopted. The new company moved away from coaches towards bus services following deregulation, but four years later, in 1990, the business closed. Seen approaching Chippenham bus station on Wiltshire County Council-funded Service 92 is National 2 ETT 319Y, which was new to the Devon Area Health Authority. (RS)

Known locally as 'the green buses', AA Motor Services were one of the famous Ayrshire co-operatives, formed by several smaller operators pooling together under one operating name and operated until June 1997, when the members sold out to Stagecoach Western Buses. A306 YSJ was new to Young's of Ayr, who were one of the more prominent members of AA. (RJ)

Just under 200 Greenways were built in the four years the project was live. While many received 'cherished' registration numbers, National 2-based AFM 1W kept its original identity. New in 1981 to Crosville as its SNL1 and used on the Runcorn busway, it was rebuilt in 1992 and entered service with Hyndburn Transport. It later passed to Eagre of Gainsborough and is seen pulling out of Gainsborough bus station on Eagre's town service. (RS)

To finish this section we have one of each standard National. This Mainline trio parked at the rear of Greenland Road garage in Sheffield consists of UPB 298S, new to London Country in 1977, KWA 27W, a National 2 new to SYPTE in 1980, and AAK 110T, a B Series that was also new to SYPTE in 1979. (RS)

The Tiger

The Tiger was introduced primarily as a premium specification coach chassis in response to the influx of high-specification Continental chassis entering the UK market. However, with the discontinuation of the Leopard, the Tiger also needed to be made suitable for bus work. The 'TRB' variant of the Tiger chassis originally had a downrated version of the TL11 engine and leaf springs in place of the usual air suspension, but was available with the same choice of manual or semi-automatic gearboxes as the coach. Operators who had previously used the Leopard for bus work were more than happy to switch to the Tiger, and from 1984 Leyland offered the Gardner 6HLXC engine, aimed primarily at the Scottish Bus Group, who had an unwillingness to use Leyland engines, much preferring Gardners. Leyland initially refused to offer the Gardner engine, but after Dennis introduced the Gardner-engined Dorchester aimed specifically at the SBG market, Leyland relented and the Patricroft product was added to the Tiger options.

Following the privatisation and division of Leyland Truck and Bus, a problem arose with engine supply, as the TL11 was built at the foundry of the truck plant and to build the small number of horizontal versions required by Leyland Bus was expensive. As a result, from 1988 the TL11 was withdrawn as an option, to be replaced by the Cummins L10 – an engine which could be rated up to 290 bhp and which was renowned for its fuel economy. Following Volvo's takeover of Leyland, the Tiger was also available with Volvo's 9.6-litre engine. The final chassis were assembled in 1991.

In days gone by when the larger industrial towns and cities had their annual shutdown, it was common for the most unlikely buses to be pressed into service on holiday express duplicates. On hire to Scottish Citylink are a pair of Wadham Stringer Vanguard-bodied Tigers from A1 Service member McKinnon of Kilmarnock, with OSJ 35X leading sister OSJ 36X through Blackpool. (MH)

Integrated bus services across West Yorkshire took a huge step in 1981 when Metrobus (West Yokshire PTE) and the West Yorkshire-based NBC subsidiaries formed the Metro-National Transport Company Limited. Buses began to appear with a new emblem consisting of the Metrobus WY in one box and the NBC double-N logo in another. Showing this to good effect while waiting time in Sheffield bus station is WYPTE's 1655 (EWR 655Y), a Duple Dominant-bodied Tiger. (RS)

With its post-privatisation livery suiting the lines of the vehicle, Midland Red (North) Duple Dominant bodied Tiger A705 HVT passes through Stafford town centre en route to Wolverhampton. It carries a Stoke-on-Trent registration as when delivered new to NBC subsidiary Midland Red fellow NBC subsidiary PMT handled their registration matters. (MH)

Hutchison of Overtown ordered eighteen Duple Dominant buses between 1977 and 1988, fitted to a variety of chassis. Only two were on Tigers, one of which was 1983-delivered OGE 9Y. It later passed to Rossendale Transport and is seen here in Corporation Street, Manchester. (RS)

Well-respected Lincolnshire operator Delaine of Bourne operate a network of services from Bourne to Spalding, Stamford and Peterborough, and are one of the few independent operators still purchasing brand-new service buses. Pictured outside the company's depot is A24 OVL, the second of five high-capacity Duple Dominant bus-bodied Tigers purchased. (SG)

The Tiger sold well in Australia, where it found use as an urban route bus or as a coach. Before purchase by Southland Bus Services of Moorabbin in 1983, PMCSA-bodied BXH 048 was a demonstrator, and was the first Tiger to enter service with a Melbourne operator, beating Ventura by four months. (Geoff Foster).

The Alexander P type was a utilitarian body built between 1983 and 1988 to replace the long-running Y type. East Midlands was the only NBC subsidiary to take any P types, 632 (B632 DWG) being one of nine delivered in 1985. It is seen approaching Doncaster South bus station at the end of the X24 from Sheffield via Maltby and Tickhill. (RS)

Having built some wonderful curvy bodies in the shape of the Y and M types, Alexander's later offerings such as the Belfast-built N type were particularly angular. Built in dual-purpose and standard form, Ulsterbus 460 (HXI 460) from 1986 is one of the former, but by the time this picture was taken in Coleraine it had been downgraded to local bus spec. (MH)

The Ministry of Defence took large numbers of Tiger buses fitted with a variety of bodies. When surplus to requirements they were placed for sale on the open market and became ideal for use on school contracts. Originally 64-KD-86 when new in 1986, Wadham Stringer Vanguard-bodied HFU 531 passed to Eagre of Gainsborough in 1996. (RS)

As well as Wadham Stringer bodies, the MOD took a large number of Plaxton Derwent 3000-bodied Tigers. Beautifully presented despite being the spare vehicle in the fleet of Paul's Coaches of Harriseahead, Stoke-on-Trent, D458 ENV was converted from manual to semi-automatic gearbox after withdrawal by the MOD. (MH)

Another operator taking an ex-MOD Plaxton Derwent-bodied Tiger was Cooper of Killamarsh. The former 03-KJ-42 originally received registration G746 FTW before acquiring cherished plate SIL 7764. Used to operate the 'Coastline Clipper', it received a set of coach seats but retained its manual gearbox. (RS)

While the majority of East Lancs-bodied Tiger buses were built on chassis that had previously carried time-expired coach bodies, a handful were also built on brand-new chassis. The sole example delivered to Lancaster City Transport was D154 THG, which was new in 1986 as fleet number 154. (MH)

While most of the Plaxton Derwent-bodied Tigers went to the MOD, twenty-five were delivered new to independent operators. E829 AWA was new to Richardson of Sheffield but lasted just over twelve months before it passed to Liverline. It is seen in Barnsley bus station when Richardson provided the X36 motorway service between Barnsley and Rotherham. (RS)

Above and below: Alexander's P type might not have been their finest in styling terms, but when it came to structural strength it was second to none. Grimsby Cleethorpes' Gardner-engined Tiger E930 PBE is seen standing at Cleethorpes Pier. In 1993, Grimsby Cleethorpes became part of the Stagecoach empire and E930 PBE went north of the border to operate with Bankfoot Buses of Perth. It subsequently travelled to the Midlands and is still operational in the fleet of Stanways of Rode Heath, on whose garage forecourt it is seen. (RS/MH)

The first Duple 300-bodied Tiger buses delivered to an English operator were seven dual-purpose vehicles for West Yorkshire PTE in 1983, a further fifteen arriving the following year. In the years following privatisation, both West and South Yorkshire PTEs became part of First Group, and after a period of time operating in Halifax, A662 KUM was transferred to the south of the county and is seen in Dinnington bus station. (RS)

Another example of 'if it has wheels let's use it' is F452 FDB, a very smart Duple 300-bodied Tiger operated by Ralph Bullock of Cheadle. Fitted with coach seats, it is pictured at the Leprechaun in Queensferry en route to Pwllheli alongside Bostock's of Congleton's Duple Goldliner-bodied Tiger. (MH)

Reversing off the stand in Gloucester bus station is Cottrell of Mitcheldean's Duple 300-bodied Tiger F309 RMH, new in 1988 to Dell (Rover Bus Service) of Chesham. (RS)

In the late 1980s, well-known tour operator Shearings entered the local bus market and supplemented its second-hand bus fleet with a batch of sixteen Alexander N-type-bodied Tigers. They were some of the last Tigers to be built and were fitted with Cummins engines and ZF automatic gearboxes. G67 RND is seen waiting time in Macclesfield bus station. (MH)

Seen when brand new in February 1986 prior to registration is the forty-one-seat dual-door Ansair bodied CRO.055, one of three similar vehicles delivered to Southland Bus Services of Moorabbin. (Bruce Tilley)

An indication of how popular the Tiger was in Australia can be seen along the side of PMC-bodied CVB.001 of Ventura Bus Lines of Melbourne. It took only three years for this milestone to be reached, and the bus is on display at the 1986 Melbourne Bus Show. (Bruce Tilley)

Another PMC-bodied Tiger is fifty-seven-seat MO.6361 delivered in 1985 to John J. Hill Bus Services of Wollongong NSW and is seen outside the Wollongong depot. One of sixteen similar buses delivered between 1985 and 1989, it has since been preserved. (Norman Chambers)

The Lynx

While the National was acknowledged as one of the most revolutionary designs of public transport in its era, advancements in technology saw Leyland's development team start work on the National's replacement in the early 1980s. Unlike the National, the Lynx was to be made available with a choice of engines from the outset, and whereas the National was an all-steel design using traditional gasket rubbers for the windows, the Lynx used bonded glazing and aluminium in the body construction. This gave a considerable improvement in unladen weight, which led to much better fuel consumption and performance. By 1984, running prototypes were being evaluated, with examples placed in large fleets including Ribble and WM Buses, which led to both operators ordering large numbers of the Lynx. Whereas the National had been an integrally constructed bus, the Lynx had a chassis, but all received Leyland's own body apart from the first batch to hit the road, which were actually sent as underframes to the Alexander plant in Belfast. Different seating and door arrangements were available, but the Lynx was only built to one length: 11.2 metres. It became apparent very early in production that nowhere near as much research and development had gone into the Lynx as did with its predecessor, and numerous warranty claims surfaced due to rust spreading through the welded box section due to poor anti-corrosion treatment of the steel frame. As with the Tiger, the Lynx was available with the TL11, Gardner or Cummins L10 engines as well as a fully or semi-automatic gearbox. The Lynx 2 arrived in 1990, the biggest visual difference being a small frontal 'nose' to make room for an intercooler, but under the surface much work had been done to eradicate the corrosion and electrical problems of the original Lynx. As the Lynx 2 was introduced after the takeover by Volvo, it was also available with the 9.6-litre Volvo engine.

By 1992 the writing was on the wall for all the pre-takeover Leyland products, and in August of that year the final Lynx rolled off the Workington production line, and just like the National before it, the final vehicle was delivered to Halton Transport. From personal experience the Lynx was a good vehicle to drive, and when fitted with the Cummins engine and ZF automatic gearbox it had acceleration far ahead of anything else in its class.

Out of all the Lynxes built, only eight didn't receive Leyland's own bodywork, and surprisingly six of these were the first complete buses delivered. Fitted with Alexander N-type bodies and Gardner engines, they were delivered to Citybus of Belfast in 1986. All subsequently passed to Stevenson's of Uttoxeter, who, post-deregulation, expanded their operations far outside their traditional East Staffordshire base. Seen having a Sunday morning lie in at the former North Western/Crosville garage in Macclesfield is HXI 3011. (MH)

Boro'line Maidstone 7 (D155 HML) was one of three delivered new to the operator in 1987. Boro'line was formed in 1986 as an arm's length company of Maidstone Borough Council, and was one of the earliest participants in the London Transport route tendering system. However, this rapid expansion as well as competition closer to home saw Boro'line Maidstone being placed into administration in February 1992, and three months later the company ceased operating. (RS)

The AA Buses co-operative ordered five new Lynxes, with member Dodds being the first independent operator to order the model. F262 WSD was a later delivery and is seen reversing off the stand at Ayr bus station on the core route to Ardrossan. (AS)

In 1988, much to the appreciation (and relief) of us coach drivers, Western National went on a buying spree and added ten brand-new executive coaches to the fleet. They also purchased six Cummins-engined Lynxes, split between the Plymouth and Cornwall divisions. The first of the batch was 200 (E200 BOD), seen at the top end of Royal Parade in Plymouth in 1990. (AS)

As seen earlier, Safeguard of Guildford were firm Leyland devotees. Guildford is also the home to rival manufacturer Dennis, who re-entered the world of bus building in the late 1970s. Eventually, Safeguard did buy Dennis products, but when photographed in 1990 there were still several Leylands operating, including Lynx E297 OMG. (AS)

West Midlands PTE operated the largest number of Lynxes, with a fleet of over 250. Six of them were ex-demonstrators fitted with semi-automatic gearboxes which were soon converted to ZF automatics. They had long service lives, with the last examples remaining in passenger service until 2009. Seen when brand new (and still in possession of its Lynx grill badge) is G245 EOG, seen on St Martin's Circus passing Manzoni Gardens, now completely eradicated by the redevelopment of Birmingham city centre. (AS)

Above and below: After having been split into separate divisions in the lead up to privatisation, the city and country divisions of what was Bristol Omnibus were brought back together again in 1988 when Midland Red Holdings, the company which had purchased the Bristol city operation from the NBC, was taken over by Badgerline, the company responsible for the country routes. Both operated Lynxes, and examples from the two fleets are seen on St James Barton roundabout in Bristol city centre. Muller Road depot-based MR1628 (F628 RTC) from the City Line fleet passes a vinyl-roofed Chrysler Alpine while working the 71 from Knowle West to Filton Church. Meanwhile, Wells-based H613 YTC is heading into Marlborough Street bus station after having worked in from its home city. (AS)

Despite taking the National by the hundreds, London Buses only ordered six Lynxes, all delivered to Shepherds Bush garage in August 1989 to replace Nationals on the 283 route. In 1990 they were transferred to Stamford Brook garage and operated under the Riverside Bus brand. LX3 (G73 UYV) was the first to be delivered and is seen turning off Hammersmith Road with the old West London Hospital in the background. (AS)

Chambers of Bures was founded in 1877 and purchased their first motorbus in 1918, building up a network of services in the Sudbury, Bury St Edmunds and Colchester areas. In 2012, Chambers was acquired by the Go-Ahead Group, but seen waiting in Sudbury bus station while the company was still in independent hands is E87 KGV, the only Lynx operated, and, like most of Chamber's buses, bought new. (AS)

Above and below: Another demonstrator was Leyland-engined F74 DCW, later immortalised in model form by Original Omnibus. It is seen here on hire to PMT in Stoke, who must have been suitably impressed as eleven were ordered in 1990. The order was originally intended to be ten Lynxes and ten DAF SB220 Optare Deltas, but the price of the DAFs resulted in an 11 to 9 order in favour of the cheaper Leyland. The Lynxes were much more popular with the drivers and returned greater fuel economy – it was alleged the 11.6-litre DAF-engined Deltas achieved 4 mpg before they were run-in. Seen after PMT became part of First Bus but before corporate identity took over, an apparently driverless 858 (H858 GRE) waits on The Avenue in Kidsgrove. (MH)

Another East Anglian independent to be acquired by the Go-Ahead Group was Hedingham Omnibuses of Sible Hedingham. Much larger than Chambers, Hedingham increased in size over the years by acquisition and by the time of the takeover was one of the biggest independent operators in the country. Seen outside the garage at Hedingham is Mk 2 Lynx L206 (J724 KBC), which was new to Westbus of Ashford in 1992. (AS)

With a fleet of thirty-one vehicles, West Riding was the largest operator of the Mk 2 Lynx. The frontal differences between the two models is evident on Mk 1 349 (G148 CHP) and Mk 2 359 (H359 WWY), seen in the long since demolished Union Street bus station in Wakefield. (AS)

The only dual-door Lynxes built were a batch of twelve Mk 2s delivered to Lothian. The last of the batch was H188 OSG, seen leaving Lothian's Central garage in Annandale Street, Edinburgh, when brand new in 1991. (AS)

Moving to South Wales, we see Mk 2 Lynx J262 UDW from the Cardiff Corporation fleet. It's travelling down Wood Street in Cardiff city centre with the corporation headquarters in the background, which if my memory (and stomach) remembers correctly had a staff canteen which produced excellent bacon rolls. (MH)